GOOD
MANNERS

Modern Publishing
A Division of Unisystems, Inc.
New York, New York 10022

CONTENTS

We Are Not Alone 4

At Home 6

Order and Disorder 8

Soap and Water 10

A Birthday Party 12

Invitations and Place Cards 14

A Treasure Hunt 15

Pies and Cookies 16

Plates and Silverware 18

Hello, Bonjour, Buenos Dias 20

Thank You, Merci, Gracias 22

Does Your Nose Grow
Like Pinocchio's? 24

Play the Game of
Good Manners 25

Rules for the Game of
Good Manners 32

The Frog Prince 33

Friendship 34

Yesterday and Today 36

Frills and Lace 38

Nature 40

Remove Your Armor 42

The ABCs of Good Manners 44

We Are Not Alone

We do not live alone on a desert
island like Robinson Crusoe. We
live with other people, and good
manners help us all get along.

At Home

Toys for Learning— Playing with a dollhouse helps you understand how to behave in your own house. In a dollhouse there is a place for everything and everything has a place. The dolls' clothing hangs in the closets, the dishes are in the kitchen cabinets, and it is much easier to move around when everything is clean and neat. This is all true for humans and their homes, too.

Animals also need to learn how to behave: cats and dogs should not climb on the furniture, or tear it with their claws.

How It Works—Everyone, old and young, can help keep a home clean. It is nice to use a bathroom that is clean and neat. Always leave it tidy for the next person. And never leave dirty dishes in the kitchen.

Indoor pets need their own corner where they can sleep quietly. They also need a place where they can always find food and water.

Respecting others means leaving each room just as you'd like to find it.

Well-Behaved—If pets are well-trained, they can go anywhere with their owners. When you take a vacation, you need to take your pets along or find a good temporary home for them.

Talking on the telephone is like going into someone else's house. When you call someone always remember to say hello and to say your name. "Hello. My name is . . . . May I speak to . . . . please? Thank you!" Always keep a pad and pencil by the telephone for taking messages.

Order and Disorder

A Magic Lamp—It would be nice to be like Aladdin: to own a genie and have him clean up your bedroom! Imagine sitting comfortably, not lifting a finger, and saying, "Put the toys in order, the books on the shelf, the clothes in the closet . . ."

Magic Tricks—To keep toys and clothing, pens and pencils, books and notebooks in order, remember to put them away right after using them. That way you will find them again easily when you want them the next time. On lower shelves keep the things you use most often. The objects you use less often can be put on the higher shelves.

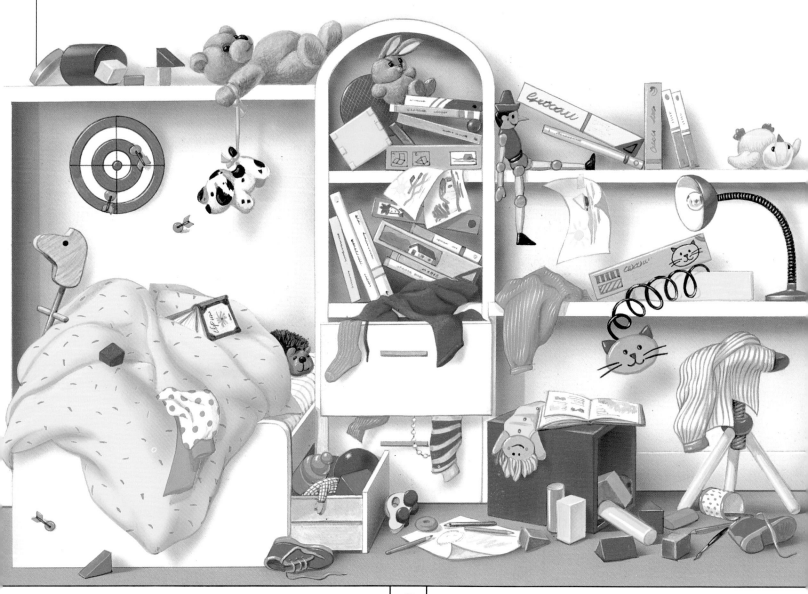

Better Than a Magic Hat—A cardboard carton can become a box for toys. You can decorate the box with markers, or peel-off stickers, or tempera paint.

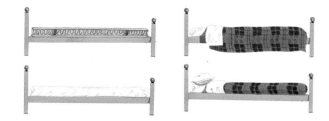

To make your bed, straighten the bottom sheet on the mattress and tuck it in. Put on the top sheet and the blanket. Leave about a foot of the top sheet sticking out beyond the blanket at the top, then fold it over the blanket. Tuck in the top sheet and the blanket at the foot-end of the bed and at the sides. Put the pillow in the pillow case and put it on the bed.

Soap and Water

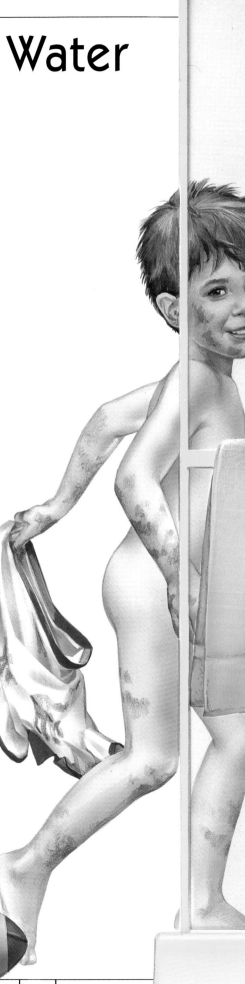

Why We Wash—Taking a bath or shower regularly, washing your hair, and brushing your teeth helps you feel good and be nice to be near.

Bubble Bath—Taking a bubble bath is a great way to relax. You can just lie in the warm water and think pleasant thoughts while you soak yourself clean.

Sea Bath—You can dissolve about 1lb of sea salt in your bath. This bath will refresh and energize you. A handful of corn starch helps to reduce skin irritations.

Your Teeth—Brush your teeth every morning and every night before bed. Before you begin to brush, floss your teeth. Always rinse your mouth well after brushing. If you take care of your teeth when you are young they will last all your life.

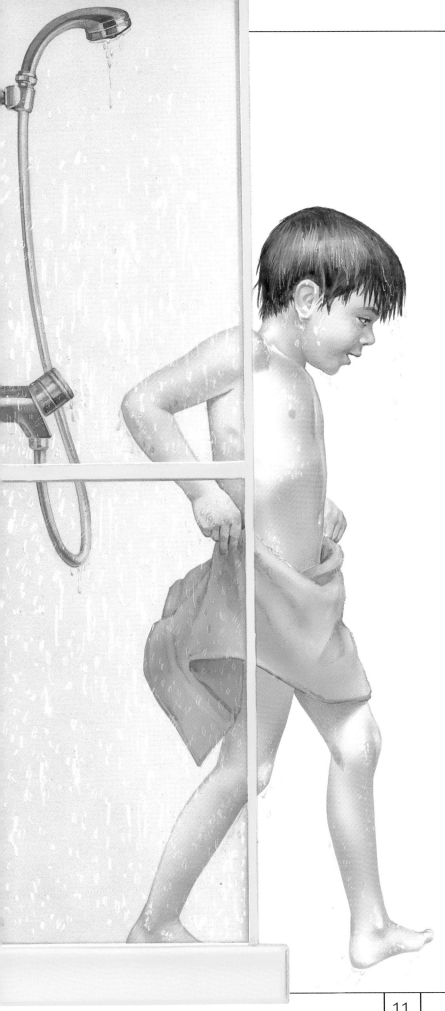

Bathroom Rules—

1. Don't stay in the bathroom too long.

2. Remember to close the door.

3. Always flush the toilet.

4. Turn off the faucets when you are done.

5. Don't leave the soap in water.

6. Hang up any towels you've used.

7. Clean the bathtub after using it.

8. Put the cap back on the toothpaste.

9. Put the toilet seat back down before you leave the bathroom.

10. Turn off the bathroom light when you leave.

A Birthday Party

Like a Cake—Having a fun party is like baking a tasty cake: you need the right ingredients. Here are some good ways to have a fun birthday party:

1. Send invitations, or tell your friends yourself at least a week before the party. Be sure to tell them where and when to show up and if special dress is needed (like a "Come as Your Favorite Person" party).

2. If the party will be outside, arrange to have a place to go in case it rains.

3. Plan so you will have enough food and drinks for your guests, and some extra, in case you have unexpected guests.

4. Make decorations for your house or yard with tissue flowers or chains of looped construction paper.

5. Welcome each guest personally.

6. Tell your neighbors ahead of time if you think the party will be noisy (then they can make other plans).

Another way to avoid complaints from angry neighbors is to invite them to the party!

Games to Play— There are many different kinds of games to play at birthday parties; which games you play depends on how many people there will be and how much space there is. You can play hide-and-seek or pin-the-tail-on-the-donkey, have a treasure hunt, or play charades, bingo, and other inside games if it is cold or rainy outside.

For a party you will need:
1. **Glasses, plates, and silverware (these can be paper and plastic— they're easier to clean up but worse for the environment)**
2. **Paper or cloth napkins**
3. **Supplies for playing the party games**
4. **Prizes for the winners**
5. **Sandwiches**
6. **Cookies and a cake**
7. **Soft drinks and juice**

Invitations and Place Cards

All You Need Is a Potato— You can use a potato to make invitations or birthday cards, place cards, stationery, or gift tags. Here is what to do: first, cut the potato in half.* With a marker, draw on the flat surface of one potato half: a flower, a heart, a boat, an animal, your initial, a star, or any shape you like. Then use a knife to cut away the potato around your design. Cut about half an inch deep, so your design is raised. Then paint your design with tempera paint. Now you can use your potato like a stamp. Press the potato onto paper and make place cards or anything you wish. If you have an inked stamp pad, you can also press your potato onto it and then stamp away!

*Always ask an adult for help when you use a knife.

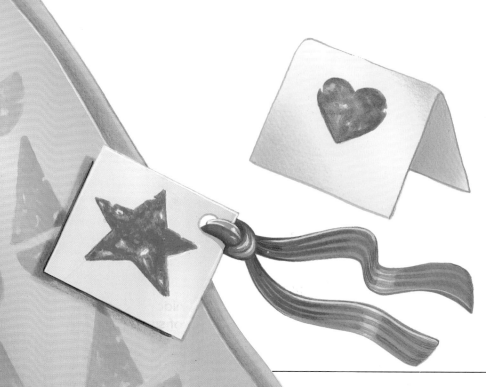

A Treasure Hunt

The book "Treasure Island" by Robert Louis Stevenson is the story of a hidden treasure, buried by pirates, that is found by following the signs on a map.

How to Organize—Treasure hunts were held centuries ago and are still a lot of fun. You can have a treasure hunt for your party. Divide your guests into two teams. The point of the game is to see which team finds the treasure first. Each team receives a card with the same first clue. For example: What runs while standing still? (Answer: Λ clock) When you guess the answer, you know where to find the second clue— near a clock! Besides having riddles as clues, a clue can also tell the team to find certain things before

they can go on to the next clue—find ten things that begin with the letter "z," find a baseball cap, or a wig, or a four-leaf clover. You can even ask a team to dress up like pirates, mummies, or scarecrows, or tie a necktie. When a team

finishes doing what a clue says, it can search for the next clue. The last clue should be a map showing where the treasure is hidden. Whichever team finds it first wins and each teammate gets a prize!

Today, hidden treasures—the cargos of sunken ships—lie at the bottom of the sea.

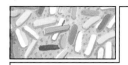

Pies and Cookies

Always get permission from an adult before you use the kitchen. Always get help when using the oven.

Recipe for Fruit Pies

You can also use this dough to make cookies.

Ingredients
1 1/4 cups of flour
1/2 cup of sugar
a pinch of salt
2/3 cup of butter
2 egg yolks
grated rind of 1 lemon
jam for filling

Set the oven at 325° F. Grease the inside of a pie plate. Put the flour, sugar, and salt into a big mixing bowl. Cut the butter into little chunks and add it to the flour, sugar, and salt. Rub the butter into the flour mixture until it looks like soft bread crumbs. Add the egg yolks. Add the lemon rind to the mixture in the bowl. Now knead everything together until it is well mixed.

Use three-quarters of the dough for the bottom of the pie. Set the rest aside to make decorations later. Roll out the bigger portion of dough with a rolling pin. When the dough is about one-quarter of an inch thick, lay it in the pan. Spread jam on the dough. Roll out the small piece of dough and cut it into strips. Decorate the top of the pie. Bake 325° F for about 30 minutes.

To Make Cookies

Roll out all the dough with a rolling pin and use cookie cutters to cut out different shapes, or you can cut your own shapes by hand. Lift the cookies with a spatula onto greased cookie sheets. Keep them at least an inch apart. They expand while they bake. Bake at 325° F for about 15 to 20 minutes.

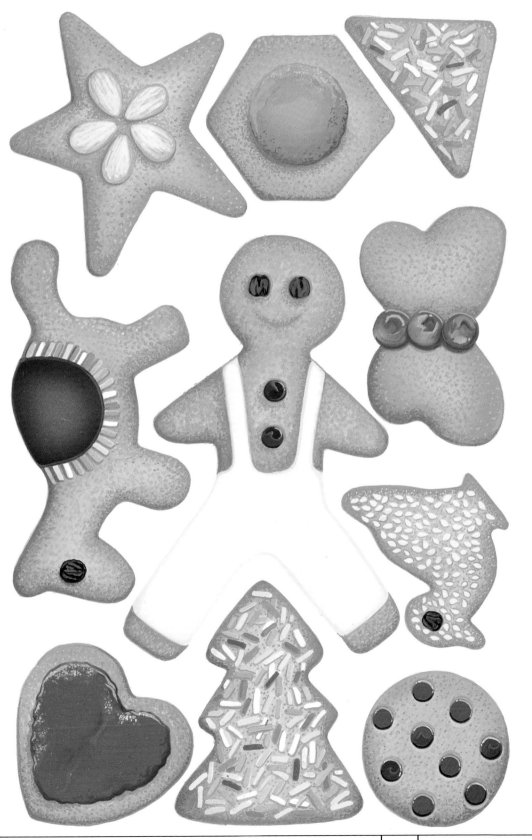

Decorating

After the cookies are baked, set them on racks to cool. When they are cool, ice them. Mix $1/2$ cup of confectioner's sugar with 1 spoonful of hot water. Spread the icing on the cookies. Before the icing dries you can decorate them with:

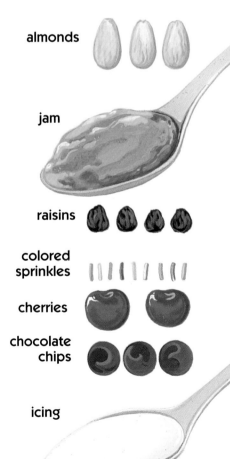

almonds

jam

raisins

colored sprinkles

cherries

chocolate chips

icing

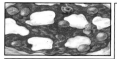

Plates and Silverware

Hands or Utensils?—In the Middle Ages, people ate with their hands, and maybe a knife or spoon. The English King Henry VIII invented forks to make eating easier and more elegant.

Water glass

Juice glass

napkin

Two forks are needed for two different courses. Use the outside fork first.

Different plates are used for different courses.

Knife and spoon

Golden rules for good table manners—

✓ Sit close to the table and sit up straight.

✓ Bring the food to your mouth, not your mouth to the plate.

✓ Keep your elbows off the table.

✓ Put your napkin on your lap and use it.

✓ Wipe your mouth before drinking from your glass.

✓ Don't clean your plate with your tongue.

✓ Ask someone politely to pass whatever you need.

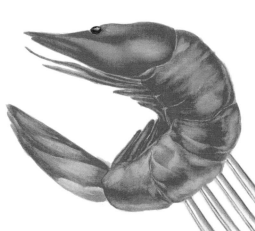

✓ Don't speak with your mouth full.

✓ Keep your elbows near your sides to avoid poking your neighbor.

✓ Put your silverware neatly on your plate when you have finished eating.

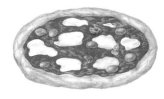

✓ Don't reach across the table.

✓ Don't pile your plate up with more food than you can eat.

✓ Ask permission to leave the table when you have finished eating.

Keeping these rules makes meals pleasant for everyone at the table.

Hello, Bonjour, Buenos Dias

Greetings from Around the World—
When you travel to a foreign country, the first and most useful word to learn is "hello." Here's how to say hello in many different languages:

English: hello
French: bonjour
Spanish: buenos dias

German: guten Morgen
Dutch: goedemorgen
Japanese: konnichi wa
Russian: dobri zién
Greek: kalimera
Italian: buon giorno
Arabic: sabâhalkhir
Chinese: zao shang hao
Zulu: sakubona

Greetings from an Eskimo—What people think are good manners can change a lot from country to country. For example, instead of shaking hands, Eskimos say hello by rubbing noses. Well-mannered Japanese always remove their shoes before entering a house. Arabs eat with their right hands. In Thailand the sole of the shoe is never seen; it's considered very impolite. Never offer a glass of wine to a Muslim; their religion does not permit them to drink alcohol.

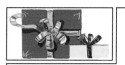

Thank You, Merci, Gracias

The Password—The secret to getting what you want is to ask for it nicely. "Please" and "thank you" are the secret words.

A Gift as a Thank You— If you have had a nice dinner at someone's house or they have done you a favor, you may want to give them a thank you gift as well as a verbal "thank you."

Gifts that have unusual shapes are hard to wrap. For a tube-shaped present, wrap it like salt-water taffy, with a bow at each end.

If a gift is tiny, you can play a trick on the person you're giving it to. Put the present in a small box. Put that box in a slightly bigger box, and so on. When you wrap your present, it will look much bigger than it really is!

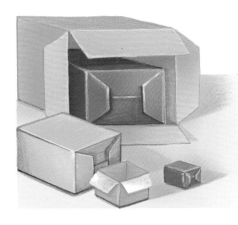

"Please" and "Thank You"—
These are very important words to know. Here is how to say them in different languages:

English: please, thank you

Japanese: dozo, domo arigato

Dutch: alsjeblieft, dankjewel

Spanish: por favor, gracias

German: bitte, danke schön

French: s'il vous plaît, merci

Russian: pojalsta, spassiba

Greek: parakalò, efkaristò

Italian: per favore, grazie

Arabic: min fadlika, shukran

Chinese: lautia, shee shee

Zulu: ngicela, ngayabonga

Does Your Nose Grow Like Pinocchio's?

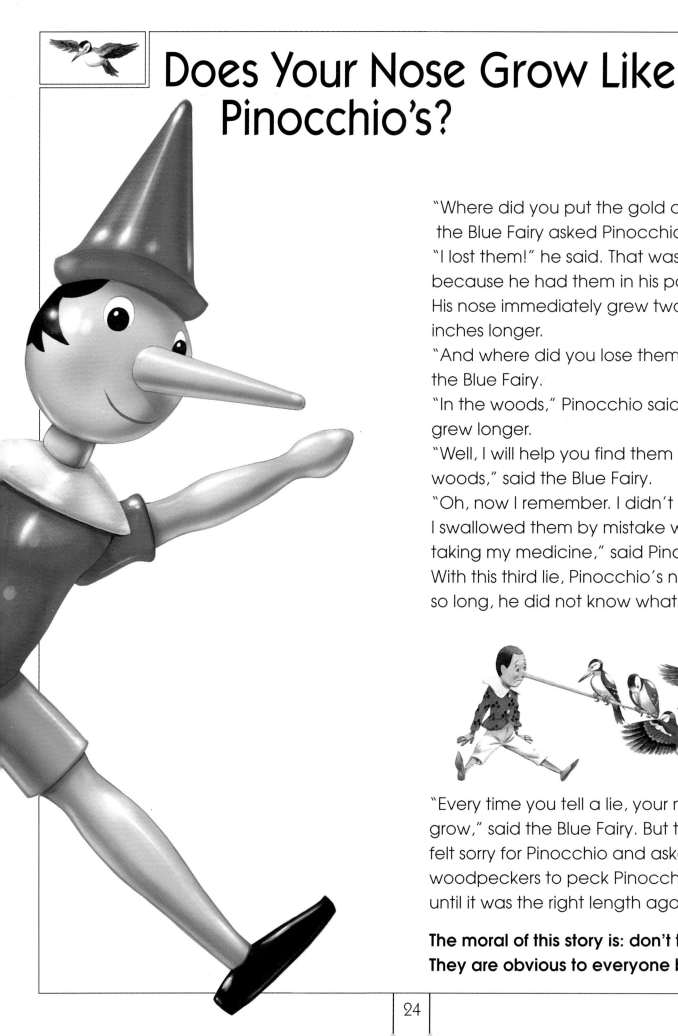

"Where did you put the gold coins?" the Blue Fairy asked Pinocchio.

"I lost them!" he said. That was a lie, because he had them in his pocket. His nose immediately grew two inches longer.

"And where did you lose them?" asked the Blue Fairy.

"In the woods," Pinocchio said. His nose grew longer.

"Well, I will help you find them in the woods," said the Blue Fairy.

"Oh, now I remember. I didn't lose them, I swallowed them by mistake when I was taking my medicine," said Pinocchio. With this third lie, Pinocchio's nose grew so long, he did not know what to do.

"Every time you tell a lie, your nose will grow," said the Blue Fairy. But then she felt sorry for Pinocchio and asked the woodpeckers to peck Pinocchio's nose until it was the right length again.

The moral of this story is: don't tell lies. They are obvious to everyone but you.

Play the Game
— *of* —
Good Manners

The rules for this game are on page 32.

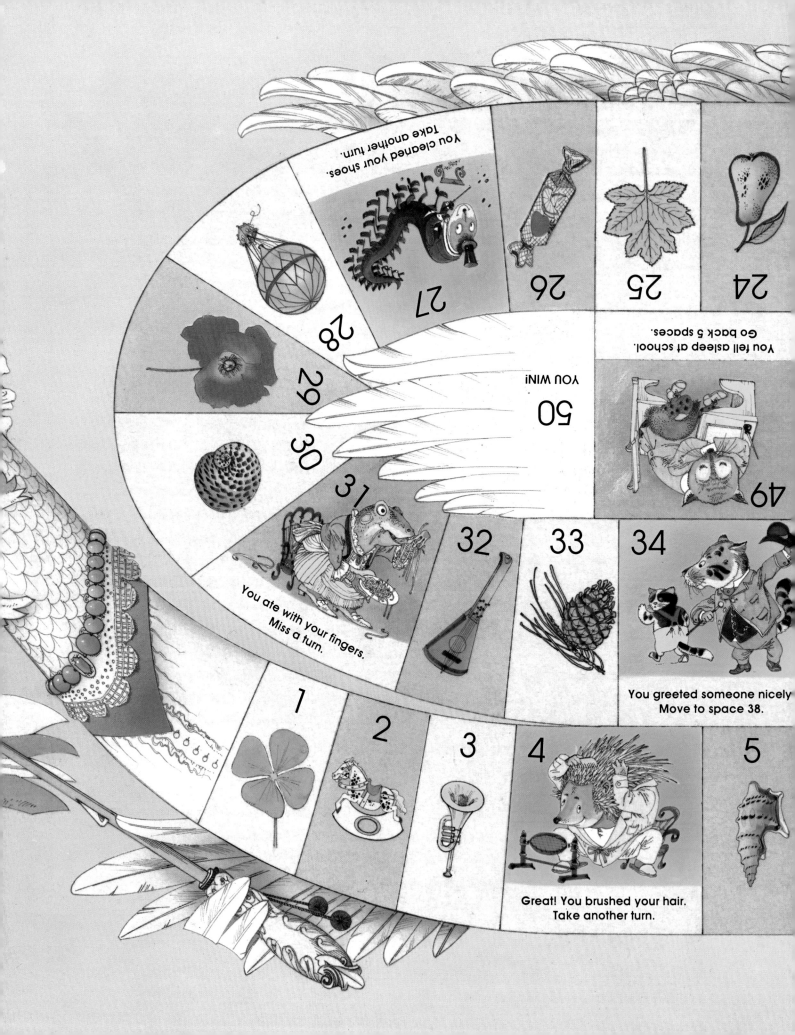

You cleaned your shoes.
Take another turn.

27

26

25

24

You fell asleep at school.
Go back 5 spaces.

YOU WIN!
50

49

28

29

30

31

32

33

34

You ate with your fingers.
Miss a turn.

You greeted someone nicely.
Move to space 38.

1

2

3

4

5

Great! You brushed your hair.
Take another turn.

Don't forget to comb your hair
before you leave for school.

Use your silverware when you eat.

When you get up in the morning,
be sure to make your bed.

Don't be late for school.

Cover your mouth when
you yawn.

When you get dressed, check
in the mirror that your buttons
are buttoned right.

Having clean and tied shoes
helps you look neat.

Turn the page to find a little goose who is

Watching someone eat with his hands is not a pretty sight.

When you meet someone you know, it's polite to say "Hello."

If your room is a total mess, you'll never be able to find what you need.

Put your trash in the garbage can, not on the ground!

Brush your teeth after breakfast and before bedtime.

Set the table correctly, and everyone will have everything they need.

Don't sleep on your desk. Save your sleeping for bedtime.

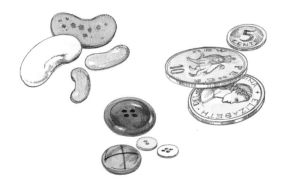

Rules for The Game of Good Manners

To play the game each player will need a marker such as a coin, a button, or a bean. You will also need a die. To decide who goes first, each player rolls the die. The one who gets the highest number goes first. Then the person on his or her left goes second, and so on. Each person rolls the die in turn and moves ahead the number of spaces shown on the die. Read the instructions that are on the space you land on. Some will tell you to move forward, backward, or skip a turn. The winner is the first player to reach the last space—number 50—with an exact roll. If you roll a number higher than the number of spaces between you and the last space, you must go back the extra number of spaces and try again next time.

Good luck!

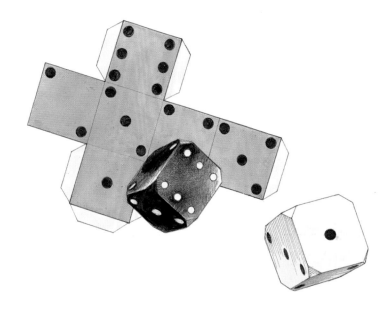

The Frog Prince

Once there was a princess whose favorite ball bounced into a pond and sank to the bottom. The princess began to cry. A big green frog hopped up and said, "I'll get your ball, Princess, if you promise that I can eat from your plate, and sleep in your bed."

"I promise," said the princess. Soon the frog was back with the ball. Without even a thank you, the princess ran off with her ball.

At lunchtime the next day, the frog arrived. He reminded the princess of her promise. She was very upset. She didn't want a frog eating off her plate. But her father said, "You must always keep a promise!" and invited the frog to stay.

From that day, the frog ate with the princess and slept in her bed At first, the princess was angry, but soon she grew to like him. One night, as she got into bed she kissed the frog good night. Suddenly there was a flash of light. The frog was now a handsome prince. The prince married the princess and they lived happily ever after.

Promises are golden. Never make a promise you don't intend to keep.

Friendship

Good and Bad Friends—Friends are people you can trust. Some people pretend to be friends, but really just want something from you—like borrowing something, or copying your math homework. A friend is someone who likes you for the person you are, not because of what you can do for them.

Friendship means caring. Remember Puss in Boots. He was a good friend. He helped his master, a poor boy, in every way he could.

Agree to Disagree—When you visit friends, they may not want to do what you want to do. You may want to watch one television program and

Snow White and the seven dwarfs were good friends. The dwarfs tried to protect Snow White from the wicked witch.

Some friends have never even met each other! They get to know each other by exchanging letters and photographs. They are called "pen pals." Often they live very far away from each other, maybe in different countries. If they speak different languages, it is a good way to practice a new language.

they may want another. They may want to eat one thing for supper when you want something else. It is good manners to respect other people's wishes, and not tell them what to do. How would you like it if your guest bossed you around in your house? Friends respect each other's differences.

Here are the five rules of friendship:
1. Keep secrets.
2. Always be honest.
3. Don't be afraid to say you are sorry for something you've done wrong.
4. Don't be a bully.
5. Share with your friends.

Who's There?—When someone rings the doorbell, be careful to find out who it is before opening the door. If your parents have told you not to open the door for anyone, be sure you obey. When the telephone rings, don't tell the caller your parents are not home. Say, "I'm sorry, my parents are busy. They can't come to the phone now. Can I take a message for them?"

Yesterday and Today

Children in Olden Days—This picture was painted in the late 1700s. It shows children of a royal Spanish family. Even though rich children then played ball and hide-and-seek, they were expected to wear tight, heavy clothing and fancy pointed shoes. Children in wealthy families also had to wear powdered wigs and bonnets with bows. Boys had to learn horseback riding and fencing as well as the usual school subjects. They also had to learn how to bow correctly and how to kiss a woman's hand. Girls were taught at home. They had to know how to embroider, how to play a musical instrument, how to curtsy, and how to dance gracefully. But not all girls were taught to read! Even though powdered wigs and curtsying have gone out of style, good manners have not. People with good manners are still the nicest people to be with.

This Family Portrait of Don Ferdinando was painted by Johann Zoffany in 1778. It is now in the Kunsthistorisches Museum in Vienna, Austria. Before cameras were invented, the only way to have a family portrait made was to pose for an artist for many days wearing your best clothing.

Frills and Lace

The Alarm Clock Rings—
It's time to get up, get dressed, and go to school. Today children are not forced to wear complicated clothes.

Old-fashioned shoes and modern sneakers

They can wear pants, shorts, long or short skirts. Children can wear sneakers or any shoes they like.

This painting of the Infanta Margarita was painted in 1659 by Velasquez. It is in the Kunsthistoriches Museum in Vienna.

Crinolines and Ruffs—
In the past children needed help to get dressed. Girls wore starched clothing supported by crinolines—stiff hoops that look like birdcages. Boys wore lacy, embroidered shirts, puffy pants, and shoes with buckles. Girls had to wear dresses all the time. Often they had lace trimmings.

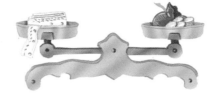

When Louis XIV was king, lace cost more than gold.

Louis XIV, king of France in the late 1700s, started the fashion of wearing lace, even on men's clothing. After a while, men's clothing became fancier and more expensive than women's. In the 1600s, both adults and children were expected to wear stiff lace collars called "ruffs."

An old-fashioned crinoline

Politeness Still Matters—
Even though modern clothing is much more comfortable and practical than it was 200 years ago, it is still important to sit up straight and have good manners.

A lace fan

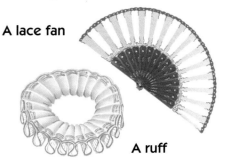

A ruff

Children do not need to curtsy or kiss hands, but they still need to say "please" and "thank you" and remember that the dinner table is not the gym.

Portrait of Little Lady Waugh, painted by William Larkin in 1615. She was about a year old when this portrait was painted.

Nature

Bean plants grow very fast, but not as fast as Jack in the Beanstalk's. In one night it grew beyond the clouds.

Good manners also grow. The more you use them the easier it is to be well mannered.

Saving the Earth—Good manners help solve the problems of pollution and the overuse of resources, so that children in the future can enjoy the earth as we do. Here are some rules that help preserve the environment:

* Don't litter. If you're on a hike, take all your garbage home with you.
* If you camp out, bring a portable stove with you. If you build a campfire, pour water on it when you are finished. Before you leave, make absolutely sure that your fire is out.
* Don't pick wild plants without permission.
* Don't waste water or electricity.
* Recycle paper, glass, aluminum, steel, and plastic whenever possible.

Grow a Plant—Where do apple and orange seeds go? What about cherry, apricot, and avocado pits? If they are thrown away, they will never grow. If you plant one in a pot with some dirt, water it often, and make sure it gets enough sun, it will grow into a plant that you can enjoy. In time the plant may bear fruit of its own!

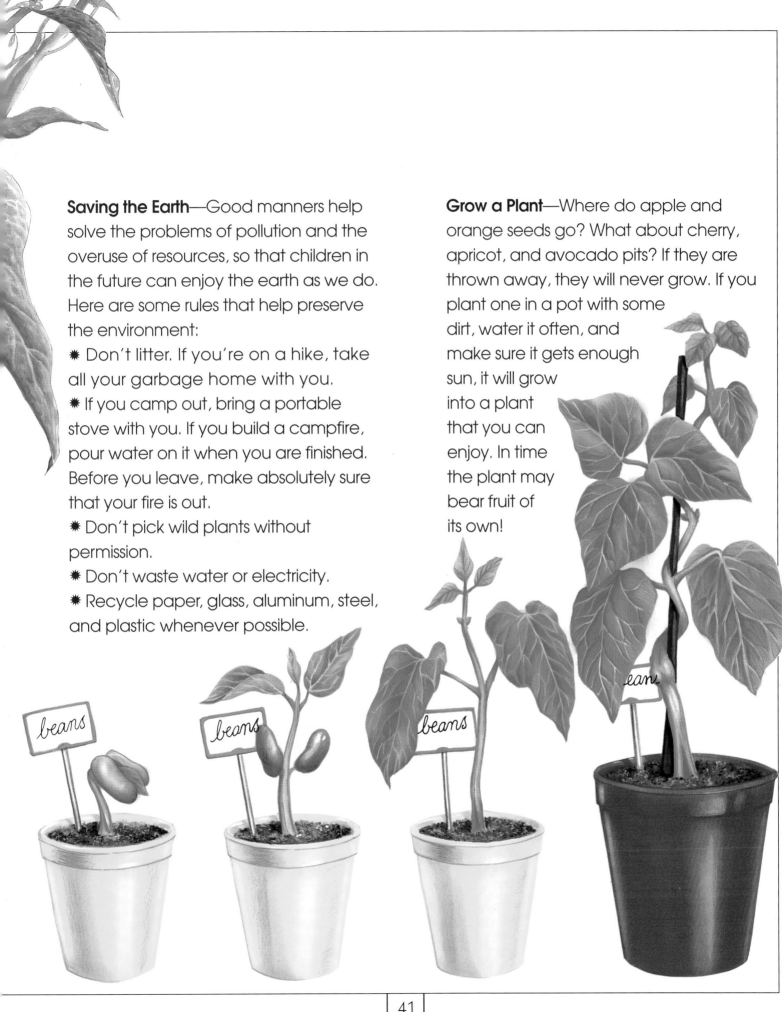

Remove Your Armor

Being Friendly—Medieval knights wore heavy armor made of metal. It was useful because it protected them from injury during combat, but it also isolated them from people who were not their enemies. We sometimes wear a kind of armor too. Invisible armor.

All you have to do is smile to make friends with someone who comes from another country.

If we are indifferent, selfish, or shy, we isolate ourselves from people around us and become insensitive to their problems and to their happiness. We must always go out of our way to be kind or friendly. And we must be ready to give help when people need it.

Families are like big oak trees with deep roots. They stand strong and make us feel safe.

The ABCs of Good Manners

Acting up—Don't act up. Be considerate of other people.

Apologize—If you do something wrong, apologize.

Appearance—If you want to look good, be sure all your buttons are sewn on, your hems are neat, there are no spots on your clothing, and your shoes are clean.

Bottle—Don't just throw empty bottles away. Always recycle.

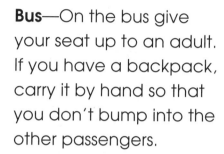

Bus—On the bus give your seat up to an adult. If you have a backpack, carry it by hand so that you don't bump into the other passengers.

Breaking—If you break something, apologize and offer to replace it if you can.

Busybody—Being a gossip is bad manners. It spreads rumors about others and makes people distrust you.

Cars—Never throw anything out the window; it's dangerous as well as rude. In some states and cities you will be fined for doing it.

Chewing—Don't chew with your mouth open.

Chewing Gum—Don't chew gum in class, or when you are talking. Always wrap gum in paper before throwing it away.

Clothes—Don't leave them on the floor. Put dirty clothes in the laundry hamper.

Desk—Don't draw, write your name, or stick chewing gum on your desk at school.

Door—Always knock before entering a room if the door is closed, and wait before entering.

Faces—Don't make faces at anyone.

Familiarity—You can be familiar with your friends and other children but not with adults you don't know. Address adults you don't know with the title Mr., Ms., or Mrs.

Fingernails—Always use a nailbrush to keep them clean. Don't bite them.

Cut them regularly with nail clippers or nail scissors.

Fingers—Don't lick them—wash them—even if they have chocolate on them!

Hair—Don't brush your hair in public or fiddle with it in public. Keep it clean and tangle free.

Hands—Always wash them before eating.

Head—Don't scratch your head in public.

Help—Offer to help around your home.

Hotels—Don't make noise in the hallways, leave the room and bathroom neat, and behave politely.

Interrupt—Don't interrupt when someone is speaking.

Wait until he or she has finished.

Lining Up—At the movies, the ski-lift, the supermarket, or waiting for the school bus, always respect a line. Wait for your turn, don't push, and don't sneak ahead of anyone else.

Movies—Stay in your seat (unless you have to leave for the bathroom) and don't talk while the movie is on.

Permission—Ask permission to use anything that doesn't belong to you.

Picking—Don't pick your nose, your ears, or your scabs.

Please—This is a magic word that helps you get what you want. Use it often.

Questions—Never ask embarrassing questions.

Remote Control—Don't hog the television remote control and make other people watch the programs you want to.

Sharing—Be generous with your things and wait to be invited before you use other people's things.

Time—Always be on time for appointments.

Touching—"Look but don't touch" is a good rule to remember in museums, stores, and other people's homes.

Towel—Always hang it up after using it.

Trash—Never throw trash on the ground.

Violence—Only people who aren't smart enough to get what they want with courtesy use insults or violence.

Visiting—You should always let people know ahead of time if you are going to visit their home.

Voices—It is rude to whisper or speak in such a low voice that others cannot hear you. Shouting is also disruptive and impolite.

Volume—A loud television or radio can bother your neighbors and your family. Always use head-phones on a train or subway. If you are wearing headphones and someone talks to you, remove them.

Wait—Nobody likes to wait, but complaining about it doesn't help. Always take along a book to read when you think you might have to wait somewhere. It will make the time go faster.

Italian text and illustrations copyright © 1993 Dami Editore.
English text copyright © 1994 Modern Publishing, a division of Unisystems, Inc.

Concept by Elisabetta Dami, Adriana Sirena

U. S. edition designed by Barbara Lipp

U.S. text by Debby Slier

Illustrated by: Simonetta Baldini, Cecilia Bozzoli, Luana Freno, Matteo Lupatelli, Elena Mandich, Rosalba Moriggia, Salvatore Palazzolo, Umberta Pezzoli, Maria Piatto, Laura Rigo, Sergio R. Rizzato, Studio Rosso

Grateful thanks to Franco Maria Ricci, Laura Ashley, and Weiss Gallery, London,
for permission to reproduce Portrait of Little Lady Waugh
(Photo by P. Cummings)

™World of Knowledge is a trademark of Modern Publishing, a division of Unisystems, Inc.
® Honey Bear Books is a trademark owned by Honey Bear Productions, Inc.,
and is registered in the U.S. Patent and Trademark office.

Printed in EEC, Officine Grafiche De Agostini - Novara 1994
Bound by Legatoria del Verbano S.p.A.